MOVING TO AMERICA

The **ULTIMATE**

BEGINNER'S GUIDE To

MAKING YOUR MOVE A SUCCESS

SUSIE LAVENDER

Legal Notice:

This book is only for personal use. This book is copyright protected under the U.S. Copyright Act of 1976 and all other applicable international, federal, state, and local laws, and all rights are reserved, including resale rights. You cannot amend, distribute, sell, use, quote, or paraphrase any part, or the content within this book, without the written permission of the author or publisher.

Disclaimer:

Although the author and publisher have made reasonable efforts to ensure that the contents of this book were correct at press time, the author and publisher do not make and hereby disclaim any representations and warranties regarding the content of the book, whether express or implied, including implied warranties of merchantability or fitness for a particular purpose.

The information provided in this guide is for educational and informational purposes only. It is not intended to be legal or financial advice. The author and publisher of this guide are not legal or financial professionals, and the information provided is based on their personal experiences and research.

The author and publisher hereby disclaim any liability to any other party for any loss, damage, or cost arising from or related to the accuracy or completeness of the contents of the book, including any errors or omissions in this book, regardless of the cause. Neither the author nor the publisher shall be held liable or responsible to any person or entity with respect to any loss or incidental, indirect, or consequential damages caused, or alleged to have been caused, directly or indirectly, by the contents contained herein.

You should seek your own advice from professional advisors, including lawyers and accountants, regarding the legal, tax, and financial implications of any transaction you contemplate. By using this guide, readers acknowledge and accept this disclaimer and agree to hold harmless the author and publisher of this guide from any and all liability, loss, or damage arising from the use, or reliance on the information provided herein.

© Copyright 2023 by Susie Lavender

All rights reserved

Title: Moving to America: The Ultimate Beginner's Guide to Making Your Move a Success by Susie Lavender

ISBN: 979-8852312365

To the dreamers and adventurers, may this guide be a valuable resource to help make your dreams a reality in America.

TABLE OF CONTENTS

Introduction..9
    What is it?...9
    Who is this guide for?..13

Chapter 1
    GETTING A CELL PHONE NUMBER...............................17
  The Prepaid Strategy..17
      Quick Tips...20
      Helpful Websites..20

Chapter 2
    SOCIAL SECURITY ADMINISTRATION (SSA)..................21
  Getting Your Social Security Number........................21
      Quick Tips...23
      Helpful Websites..24

Chapter 3
    OPENING A BANK ACCOUNT...25
  Banking Bonanza: Unlocking the Vault......................25
      Quick Tips...26
      Helpful Websites..27
      International Money Transfers.............................28
      Helpful Websites..28
      Getting a Credit Card – Importance of Your
      Credit Score..28

Quick Tips..29
Helpful Websites..31

Chapter 4
DEPARTMENT OF MOTOR VEHICLES (DMV)..................33
Once Upon a Time at the DMV...................................33
Quick Tips..36
Helpful Websites..37

Chapter 5
FINDING ACCOMMODATIONS..39
The Housing Hunt...39
a) Renting..41
Quick Tips..42
Helpful Websites..43
b) Buying...45
Closing Costs..46
Helpful Websites..47

Chapter 6
SCHOOLS...49
Education Avenue...49
Public schools...49
Charter schools..50
Private schools...51
Homeschooling..51
Helpful Websites about Homeschooling................55
Community Colleges..56
Colleges..57
Universities..57
Student Loans and Financial Aid............................58
Quick Tips..60
Helpful Websites..61

Chapter 7
  HEALTH INSURANCE..63
   Navigating the Health Insurance Maze.....................63
      Cost..64
      Enrolling..67
      Medicaid vs. Medicare..68
      Insurance Coverage..69
      HMO vs. PPO..70
      Quick Tips...71
      Helpful Websites...73

Chapter 8
  BUYING OR LEASING A CAR...75
   On the Road to Automotive Bliss...............................75
      Quick Tips...77
      Helpful Websites...78
   Car Insurance..78
      Helpful Websites...80

Chapter 9
  RESUME & COVER LETTER..83
   The Job Jungle: Resumes, LinkedIn, and Landing that Dream Job...83
      Quick Tips...84
      Helpful Websites...85

Chapter 10
  STARTING A BUSINESS...87
   Unleashing Your Entrepreneurial Spirit.....................87
      When to Open or Close a Business..........................89
      Helpful Websites...89
      Which Structure is Best..90

    Helpful Websites..90
    Creating a Business Plan..91
    Funding Your Business..91
    Registering Your Business..91
    Networking and Marketing...92
    Continuing Education..92
    Helpful Websites..92

Chapter 11
BUYING FOOD..93
Unveiling the Culinary Maze...93
    USDA Organic vs. Non-GMO....................................95
    Quick Tips...96
    Helpful Websites..98

Conclusion..101

INTRODUCTION

What is it?

Welcome to the ultimate guide to settling in the United States! If you're feeling overwhelmed about starting your new life in America and need a simple, straightforward, and engaging step-by-step manual on what to do first, second, and beyond, then you're in the right place. This guide has been carefully crafted to provide you with quick and essential information, ensuring you get off to a smooth start and establish a strong foundation for your exciting journey in the US.

My name is Susie Lavender, and you might be wondering, "Why should you listen to me about moving to the US?" Well, allow me to share a bit about my journey. Many moons ago, I made the bold move of relocating to the United States, and let me tell you, it wasn't a walk in the park. As I embarked on this journey, I realized a crucial lesson: there was a serious lack of comprehensive online resources that covered all the necessary steps and strategies to avoid those pesky, costly mistakes, all in one place. Practical matters that are often overlooked or not widely discussed require our attention because they cannot be avoided.

After witnessing a few close friends struggle, like me, with readjusting to life in the US and seeking my advice on how to navigate various situations, I decided to take matters into my own hands. That's when the idea for this book was born. You see, so many people from all walks of life make the leap to the US only to find themselves overwhelmed and stressed due to the country's complexity. And trust me, I'm not just talking about the financial side of things, I mean *everything*.

Armed with my own tried-and-tested experiences, I put together a complete starter guide just for you. A guide that would simplify the process step by step, provide the right resources, and help you tackle the multitude of tasks involved in settling down and starting that exciting new chapter of your life.

So here it is, my offering to make your journey a smoother one. With the lessons I've learned and the mistakes I've made (and there were many), I want to make sure that you have the knowledge and guidance you need to avoid those pitfalls and start off your new journey on the right foot. Together, let's pave the way to a seamless and fulfilling relocation experience.

I've condensed this guide into eleven chapters to keep it concise, allowing you to access the information you need quickly. But don't worry, I haven't sacrificed any entertainment value along the way. I've sprinkled in some handy tips and strategies to make your reading experience enjoyable and enlightening. The guide isn't like any other guide; it's your trusted companion, ready to assist you as you take those crucial first steps in the land of endless opportunities.

It's important to note that this guide won't walk you through the immigration process.

> → If you need legal advice tailored to your specific immigration case, reaching out to the Consulate of your country in the United States is a vital step. Contact them and inquire if they can provide you with a list of

immigration lawyers they can refer you to or have on file. They can likely offer a few names, some of whom may even speak your native language and possess knowledge of the immigration intricacies between the United States and your country of origin, as these can vary significantly. It's important to remember that immigration matters are complex and unique, and this guide does not cover them. Seeking professional legal assistance is advised for navigating the complexities of immigration law.

Instead, this guide is designed to be your go-to resource once you have obtained the proper visa and are ready to embark on your American adventure. Think of it as your practical toolkit filled with invaluable insights to help you navigate the hurdles ahead.

And here's the best part: by following these tried-and-true steps, you'll not only settle in quickly but also avoid the costly missteps that I, myself, made. Consider this guide your insider's scoop, giving you an edge as you start your journey toward a fulfilling life in the United States.

Who is this guide for?

Whether you've just received your working or student visa and are embarking on your first journey to the United States, are a new green card holder, or a long-time expatriate planning to come back – or born on US soil, raised overseas and returning as adults – this guide is tailor-made for you.

I'm here to share with you the invaluable insights and lessons I learned from my own experiences. Together, we will navigate the intricacies of starting your new life in the US, ensuring that you avoid the mistakes I made. From the seemingly straightforward tasks of grocery shopping and acquiring a cell phone number to the complex challenges of obtaining a driver's license, finding health insurance, and even starting your own business, I've got you covered. Believe me when I say that adjusting to life in the US can sometimes feel like unraveling a multi-dimensional puzzle. But with me by your side, armed with confidence and a dash of humor, you will be well-prepared to conquer whatever comes your way and thrive.

Let me share a story about my friend Kelly, who embarked on her own adventure when she left Philadelphia for Paris at the age of 18. Three decades flew by, and when she returned the country was very different from the one she had left.

It was challenging for her to begin a new chapter because she had to reacquaint herself with the system. She didn't have a credit card, navigating the local grocery store was a mystery, and adapting to this new chapter in her life proved daunting. It was during this time that Kelly reached out to me, realizing the scarcity of available information online to help her settle into her newfound home in California, all conveniently compiled in one document. And now, I am here to provide that missing piece for you.

Before we embark on this exhilarating journey, brace yourself for America's notorious "fine print" and the labyrinth of added sales tax and fees. Those sneaky hidden charges have a knack for appearing out of thin air, catching you off guard at the most inconvenient moments. And let's not forget the complexities of sales tax, which vary from state to state and are often omitted from the price tag, leaving you bewildered. Calculating it can become a mind-boggling puzzle.

Moreover, the customary act of tipping at restaurants or cafes can leave you second-guessing yourself, where suggestions nudge you toward an automatic 20% gratuity. Should you tip before or after tax? The tipping culture in America can be overwhelming. Remember, while it's important to support hardworking hospitality staff, tipping should always be fair to the service received and within your means.

But fear not, for I have the ultimate solution to uncover the true cost and sidestep these financial pitfalls: ask questions!

Don't hesitate to seek clarification and safeguard your hard-earned money. If something seems unclear, take a moment to pause and reflect. It's better to err on the side of caution than to find yourself entangled in a situation that drains your wallet.

Assuming your paperwork is in order, you are now poised to conquer the United States. But where should you even begin? Perhaps your job or company dictates your destination, leaving little room for choice. However, even if you have some flexibility in selecting your new location, it's crucial to keep your budget in mind.

Some states carry a hefty price tag, and taxes—whether income, sales, or property—can vary significantly. So before you start packing your bags and booking your flight, let's ensure you have crunched the numbers and crafted a solid financial plan.

My advice: it is essential to get a local cell phone number right away. Without it, you won't be able to book the necessary appointments or get callbacks. In today's world, resources are online and if you want to snatch that great apartment you spotted online, you need to be able to call the management company right away. Administrations will often ask for a number they can reach you at, too. And I'll also add that if you do not have family, friends, and/or don't know anyone and will be hopping from place to place, I suggest you get a PO box as well even for a month or two (see Quick tips and Helpful Websites section in Chapter 2), so you can have a stable address for a while where you can get and centralize in one place all your mail and important documents like your Social Security card.

With that, let's dive headfirst into the captivating world of living in America so you can build the life you've always dreamed of.

CHAPTER 1

GETTING A CELL PHONE NUMBER

The Prepaid Strategy

Welcome to the exciting world of cell phone plans in the US! Upon your arrival, one of the first things you should get is a local number.

Now, I know what you're thinking. Other steps might appear more crucial at first, like obtaining a Social Security number rather than getting a phone number. But let me tell you, getting a cell phone number right from the get-go was incredibly helpful for me. Having a US number from the very beginning made my life a whole lot easier when it came to finding a place to live, securing transportation, contacting administrations, and more. It's like having a key that unlocks countless opportunities and simplifies your transition into this new chapter of your life. It's all part of embracing the American way of life and making connections. So don't underestimate the power of getting a cell phone number early on—it's a game-changer!

At the very start, I chose to get a prepaid number. It turned out to be a great choice because I wasn't tied to a specific plan, and I didn't need a Social Security number either. This gave me the flexibility to explore different options and figure out which plan would suit me best.

Years ago, I met someone who had won the green card lottery and arrived in Los Angeles. He chose the same strategy. After a few weeks, he realized that New York City was where he wanted to be, so he packed up and headed there. He even changed his phone number and got one with a NYC area code. What is an area code? An area code is a numerical code used in telecommunication systems to designate a specific geographic region. It helps route telephone calls to the appropriate destination based on the location of the caller or recipient. It's the first three numbers of the entire number. Since we now have smartphones, these seemingly aren't as important anymore, but some people may want to have a number that represents a particular area in the city they live in. For example, 310 for the Westside of Los Angeles or 323 for Hollywood. It's all about personal preference.

But here's the beauty of the prepaid strategy: it gives you ultimate flexibility. Once you've decided on the plan that best suits you, you can even keep the same number or switch it up, whichever you prefer. It's a win-win situation. So, keep the prepaid option in mind as you navigate the world of cell phones. It allows you to stay flexible and find the perfect fit without hassle.

Fortunately, there's no shortage of options available, ranging from major carriers like T-Mobile, Sprint, AT&T, and Verizon to Google Fi and smaller, more adventurous operators – many of whom have prepaid options. With such a wide array of choices, you're sure to find a plan that perfectly suits your needs.

However, be prepared for a potential sticker shock when it comes to the cost of cell phone plans in the US, especially compared to Europe. And if you find yourself making international calls frequently, the expenses can quickly add up.

But there are clever ways to save your hard-earned cash. For instance, you can inquire about the cost-per-minute for international calls and explore various applications that offer international calling options (Whatsapp, Viber, etc.). For instance, T-Mobile offers an international call option for an extra $15 a month, instead of the $3 per minute to call overseas, and the cost per minute can rise even more for certain locations. Depending on your needs, this is something to think about. Note that this is an option you can take for a month and cancel whenever you want, offering you even more flexibility, so just ask about it before signing up. And if you're feeling a bit nostalgic, you might even consider getting a calling card for a touch of old-school charm.

Now you may be wondering, "How do I navigate this sea of options and find the perfect plan?" The web is your trusted companion on this quest! Several websites can assist you in comparing plans, providers, and coverage areas. Consider checking out WhistleOut.com, BestPhonePlans.net, PrepaidCompare.net, and CoverageCritics.com.

Armed with a bit of research, you'll be chatting and texting away in no time! Happy dialing!

Quick Tips

1. Compare different plans and offers from each carrier to find the one that best suits your needs and budget.
2. You can also buy a prepaid SIM card if you're unsure about committing to a long-term contract.
3. A few things to be on the lookout for:

- Data: Evaluate the amount of data you will need
- Roaming and international usage: ask about the associated costs and fees. International calls can be pricey and are usually charged per minute. Therefore, do not hesitate to ask questions
- Watch out for extra and hidden fees
- Take advantage of special offers: sometimes signing up for a new plan can entitle you to a free phone
- Family plans: A good way to stay connected for less than each having their own separate plan

Helpful Websites

https://www.whistleout.com/
Compare cell phone plans and providers.

https://www.bestphoneplans.net/
Provides reviews of cell phone plans and providers.

https://prepaidcompare.net/
Helps you compare prepaid cell phone plans.

https://coveragecritic.com/
Provides coverage maps and customer reviews of cell phone providers.

CHAPTER 2

SOCIAL SECURITY ADMINISTRATION (SSA)

Getting Your Social Security Number

Unless you already have one, it's time to get your Social Security Number! If you're a newbie to the USA, you'll need to visit the Social Security Administration first thing in the morning - trust me on this one. Look up the closest office on their website and make sure to bring your passport or ID with you, with proper documents like visas, green cards, or immigrant visas in your passport, etc. depending on your situation.

It's important to note that the SSA has specific requirements for obtaining a Social Security card, and these guidelines may vary depending on your individual circumstances. To get accurate and up-to-date information on how to apply for a Social Security card, it is recommended to visit the official SSA website at www.ssa.gov or contact the SSA directly at 1-800-772-1213.

The good news is that the staff is usually pretty friendly. And let me tell you, you'll need this number for a bunch of things, so don't delay this step.

I advise you to visit a local SSA office in person to apply for your Social Security number. They should be able to provide you with the number on the same day, allowing you to get the ball rolling right away and look for work right after, if your visa allows. The card itself takes about 10 days to arrive by mail.

It's crucial to have a valid mailing address where you can receive your Social Security card. If you're staying in a temporary accommodation, consider asking a family member, friend, or someone you know if you can use their address. Alternatively, if you don't have any personal connections in the area, consider getting a mailbox at a UPS store or a P.O. Box at the nearest post office (USPS) before going to the SSA. Keep in mind that even if you're staying at a hotel, you can use its address to receive your Social Security card. The key is to ensure that you have a reliable mailing address where you can receive your important documents.

Congratulations on getting your Social Security number! Now, you're one step closer to getting your driver's license or ID. However, don't make the mistake of heading straight to the DMV (Department of Motor Vehicles) during lunchtime - that's a recipe for disaster.

Let's just say DMV locations can get pretty crowded. And by crowded, I mean seriously packed to the brim with people. It's an experience that's hard to describe unless you've been there yourself. But don't worry, I've got a helpful tip for you: book an appointment online. If you can, aim for an early morning slot so you can get it done earlier and save valuable time and sanity!

If you're feeling brave and don't want to waste any time, consider opening a bank account next.

Quick Tips

1. Apply for a Social Security Number (SSN) as soon as possible: Your SSN is your key to many services such as employment, banking, and government benefits. Applying for an SSN is free, and you can do it in person at a Social Security Administration office or online (in-person is what I suggest).

2. Find the nearest Social Security Administration office: You can use the Social Security Administration's office locator tool to find the nearest office to you. Be sure to check the office's hours of operation before you go, and arrive early to avoid long wait times.

3. Bring the necessary documents: To apply for an SSN, you will need to bring your passport or other government-issued identification, as well as documentation of your immigration status (if applicable).

4. Check the status of your SSN application: You can check the status of your SSN application online using the Social Security Administration's online tracking tool. This will help you stay informed about when your SSN will arrive in the mail.

5. Protect your SSN: Your SSN is a valuable piece of information that should be kept private. Be careful about sharing it with others, and do not carry your SSN card with you unless you need it for a specific purpose.

6. Get help if you need it: If you have questions or need assistance with your SSN application or benefits, you can contact the Social Security Administration's toll-free number at 1-800-772-1213. You can also visit the SSA website for more information and resources.

Helpful Websites

1. Social Security Administration website:
   https://www.ssa.gov/

2. Social Security Administration office locator:
   https://secure.ssa.gov/ICON/main.jsp

3. Social Security Administration online tracking tool:
   https://www.ssa.gov/myaccount/statement.html

4. Social Security Administration toll-free number:
   1-800-772-1213.

5. United States Postal Service - USPS PO Boxes website:
   https://www.usps.com/manage/po-boxes.htm

6. The UPS Store - PO Boxes website:
   https://www.theupsstore.com/mailboxes

I particularly like the UPS Store Box (called "mailbox"), because unlike a P.O. Box, you'll get a real street address for your very real small business or yourself. You can receive packages and mail from all shipping carriers and you'll have 24-hour access to your mailbox at many locations. If you are going to move from place to place in the beginning, it is also a great way to centralize all of your mail. Plus, they have small business services on hand to help you.

As for the USPS location, their hours may vary so you need to check that before signing up with them and directly at the location.

CHAPTER 3

OPENING A BANK ACCOUNT

Banking Bonanza: Unlocking the Vault

When it comes to banking in the US, there are tons of options to choose from! If you already have an account with a bank that has branches in the US (Citibank, HSBC Bank...), then you are already in a good starting place. Some overseas banks even have partnerships with US banks, so that's something to look into as well (ie. Barclays and BNP Paribas both have a partnership/agreement with Bank of America). But really, the decision is yours. Just make sure you bring your ID and social security number (if you have one).

Now, for you international students out there, don't worry if you don't have a social security number. With your passport and visa, you should still be able to open a bank account. However, it is highly recommended to consult a legal advisor as part of your plan to study overseas to verify any recent rules and regulations that apply to your specific situation.

But here's a little insider tip for you all - if you join a union down the road (depending on your field of interest), you might be able to access a Credit Union bank. These smaller institutions often offer great rates, so it is worth checking out. And the best part: once you join, your spouse and children can also open accounts there. Trust me, your wallet will thank you later!

Quick Tips

1. Research online: Before going to a bank, do some research online to find out which bank offers the best options for you. Check for banks that offer free checking accounts, no-fee ATM withdrawals, and low minimum balances.

2. Bring the required documents: Make sure to bring your ID, proof of address (utility bill, lease agreement or letter stating your temporary address), and your Social Security number (SSN) if you have one.

3. Credit unions: As mentioned previously, credit unions are a great option for banking. They often have lower fees and better interest rates than traditional banks. You may need to join a union first to open an account at a credit union.

4. Online banks: Online banks like Chime are gaining popularity for their no-fee accounts and higher interest rates. They don't have physical branches, but you can do all your banking online or through an app.

5. Choose a convenient location: If you need to visit the bank in person, make sure to choose a location that is convenient for you. Consider the distance from your home, work, or school.

6. Ask about account options: Don't be afraid to ask the bank representative about different account options that might be available to you. Some banks offer special accounts for students, veterans, or senior citizens.

7. Read the fine print: Make sure to read the terms and conditions of the account you're opening. Look for any fees, minimum balances, or restrictions that might apply.

Helpful Websites

- https://www.nerdwallet.com/
  NerdWallet is a website that offers financial advice and reviews on different banking options.

- https://www.bankrate.com/
  Bankrate offers tools and resources for finding the best bank accounts, credit cards, and loans.

- https://www.mybanktracker.com/
  MyBankTracker offers reviews and ratings of different banks, as well as a guide to opening a bank account.

International Money Transfers

Looking to transfer funds from abroad to the US? Good news! You have several options at your fingertips. One way is to make an international transfer from your foreign bank directly to your new US account. This method ensures a direct and secure transfer of funds.

Another convenient option is to use trusted websites like Wise (wise.com/us) or OFX (ofx.com/en-us). These platforms specialize in international money transfers, offering competitive exchange rates and user-friendly interfaces. Remember my friend Kelly? She uses Wise and is very pleased with the service.

So whether you prefer the traditional bank route or the convenience of online options, you have the power to move your money across borders with ease.

Helpful Websites

- https://wise.com/us/
- https://www.ofx.com/en-us/

Getting a Credit Card – Importance of Your Credit Score

Let's get down to the nitty-gritty of credit cards. I'll share my personal experience with you. When I opened a bank account,

I chose Bank of America. Excited to start building my credit, I thought it would be a good idea to apply for a credit card online right away.

Well, let me tell you, I received a letter of refusal a few days later, and I was puzzled. I headed to my branch and had a chat with a branch associate, and that's when I realized I had done it backward. They kindly explained that it's better to apply for a credit card in person at the branch when it is your first card. They provided valuable advice and also assisted me throughout the application process. Following their guidance, I applied for a secured credit card, with a $100 credit line and required a $100 deposit. I know what you might think, "Am I a child with a piggy bank?" But trust me, it's only temporary, a few months at most, and it's a great way to start establishing your credit history. Once you've built some credit, you can return to the branch and explore more "grown-up" options. There's a way to approach the system and by following these tips and using the websites provided, you can make informed decisions about getting a credit card and managing your credit score, which will help positively impact your financial well-being down the road. Think mortgage loans, real estate investments, etc.

Quick Tips

Here are some tips to keep in mind when applying for a credit card:

1. Start with a secured credit card: If you're just starting to build your credit or have a poor credit score, consider a secured credit card. You'll need to make a deposit that

is used as collateral for the credit card limit. If you use it responsibly, it can help improve your credit score.

2. Compare offers: Credit card offers come with all sorts of perks and fees. Use websites like NerdWallet or CreditCards.com to compare different offers and find the one that best fits your needs.

3. Pay on time: One of the most important factors in building and maintaining a good credit score is paying your credit card bill on time. Set up automatic payments or reminders to make sure you never miss a payment.

4. Keep your credit utilization low: The percentage of your available credit that you're using is your credit utilization. Keep it below 30% to help improve your credit score.

5. Check your report: Keep an eye on your credit report for errors or fraudulent activity. You can get a free copy of your credit report once a year from each of the three major credit-reporting agencies at AnnualCreditReport.com.

6. Know your credit score: Don't go in blind! You can check your credit score for free online at websites like Credit Karma, or through online banking.

7. Ask for help: If you're struggling with debt or have questions about your credit score, seek help from a credit counseling agency or financial advisor. Also, certain banks, like credit unions, can offer competitive consolidation loans.

Helpful Websites

- https://www.creditcards.com/
- https://www.nerdwallet.com/
- https://www.creditkarma.com/

Now that you've got your bank account squared away, it's time to tackle the Department of Motor Vehicles, aka the DMV. Buckle up, because this can be a wild ride, especially if you're in a big city. But don't let that get you down - think of it as an adventure! Just make sure you bring plenty of snacks and water, and maybe a good book (like this guide) to pass the time.

CHAPTER 4

DEPARTMENT OF MOTOR VEHICLES (DMV)

Once Upon a Time at the DMV

Ah, the dreaded Department of Motor Vehicles. No matter where you are in the United States, the DMV can be a bit of a hassle, especially in big cities. But when it comes to obtaining your driver's license (DL) or Identification card (ID card), there is simply no way around it.

The process of getting your license or ID card may vary depending on the state you're in. In most cases, you'll need to visit a local DMV office in person. Thankfully, many states now offer online services to make the process a bit more manageable.

If you're a new resident, you'll likely need to obtain an ID card or driver's license, especially if you plan on driving. Even if driving isn't on your agenda, having a valid ID card is still important.

If you only need an ID card, consider making an appointment at a DMV in a smaller nearby town. For example, the Palm Springs DMV could be a great alternative if you find yourself in Los Angeles. It's just a two-hour drive away, and you'll save yourself the headache of dealing with the crowded Los Angeles area DMVs. Plus, you can turn it into a pleasant day trip and explore the charming town. Opting for an ID card instead of a driver's license saves you from having to go back for a driving test, which can be a hassle depending on your schedule and family commitments.

To kickstart the process, you'll need to schedule an appointment either online or by phone. Depending on your location, you might have to wait a few weeks before securing an appointment. Make sure to gather all the necessary documents, including proof of residency and identification, and bring them with you when you visit the DMV.

Prepare yourself for a potentially long wait upon arriving at the DMV. It's not uncommon to spend several hours there, so bring a book or something to keep yourself entertained. Additionally, there will be an application fee to be paid, the amount of which will vary depending on your state.

When your turn finally arrives, you'll likely need to pass a vision test and, depending on your state's requirements, possibly a written test. If you're applying for a driver's license, don't forget to bring proof of insurance for the vehicle you'll be using during the driving test.

When I was preparing for my driving test, I had a misconception. In some European countries, like France, you don't use your own vehicle for the test. So I arrived at the DMV without a car, assuming I would be using one provided by them with an instructor by my side. Well, I quickly realized I was mistaken. The very few people I knew back then needed their cars to go to work, so borrowing one that day wasn't an option. However, luck was on my side. As I was discussing my predicament with a DMV officer, a kind-hearted driving school owner overheard our conversation. He came forward and generously offered his car for me to use during the test. It was a lifesaver! Thanks to his kindness, I didn't have to reschedule and received my driver's license right then and there. It's amazing how a stranger's act of kindness can truly make a difference.

If you can't find a kind soul to lend you their car for your driving test, renting one is a good option. Just verify that the vehicle has up-to-date registration and adequate insurance, and you'll be ready to tackle your driving test.

So plan accordingly and familiarize yourself with the rules of the road and practice your driving skills beforehand. You should always check your state's DMV website for detailed information regarding the process and specific requirements. Remember to maintain patience and courtesy throughout your DMV experience. The staff is just doing their job, and being polite and understanding can make the process smoother and faster for everyone involved.

Quick Tips

1. Check the DMV website for information: Before your visit, check the DMV website for requirements, forms, and available online services.

2. Know the hours of operation: Check the DMV office's operating hours, including weekends and extended hours.

3. Book your appointment online: Visit your state DMV website to schedule your appointment online to save time. Choose the correct appointment type (ID, DL, or car registration) and select a convenient date and time.

4. Prepare your documents in advance: Bring essential items such as your ID, passport, social security number, proof of residency, and other relevant papers. Check the DMV website for a detailed list of required documents.

5. Study for the written test: If you're applying for a driver's license, prepare for the written test. Download the driver handbook from the DMV website and utilize online practice tests for better preparation.

6. Bring a vehicle for the driving test: If applying for a driver's license, bring a vehicle in good condition with proof of insurance and up-to-date registration. The vehicle can belong to anyone willing to let you use theirs for your test.

7. Utilize online services: Take advantage of the DMV website's online services to save time and effort. Services such as car registration renewal, address change, and ordering a replacement ID or DL can be conveniently completed online.

8. Consider smaller DMV offices: Research and find smaller DMV offices near you, as they may be less crowded.

9. Be patient: DMV offices can be busy with long wait times, so bring something to do and be patient and respectful toward the staff.

Helpful Websites

- DMV office locator (all states):
  https://www.dmv.org/dmv-office-finder.php
  DMV.org is your go-to for DMV services. Note this website is private and **NOT** operated by any state government agencies.

- https://www.ace.aaa.com/
  AAA members can access certain DMV services at AAA offices, like car registration, saving time and hassle.

- https://driving-tests.org/
  Offers free practice tests for the written DMV exam with instant feedback on answers.

- Examples of Official DMV websites:

  California: https://www.dmv.ca.gov/
  New York: https://dmv.ny.gov/

CHAPTER 5

FINDING ACCOMMODATIONS

The Housing Hunt

Looking for a new place to live can be a daunting task. Believe me, I've been there. It all depends on your budget, family situation, and if you have a furry friend or two. But don't worry, as online resources can help you out. Here are some tips to help you find the perfect place:

- → If you have children, finding a good school is important (see Chapter 6). Research the different types of schools, including public, private, and charter schools, as well as homeschooling options. Consider the curriculum, reputation, and cost of each option. Useful websites like greatschools.org can provide helpful information on school ratings and reviews.

→ For single people or couples without children, the choice is yours.

Do your research ahead of time and consider the costs of living in different cities and your personal situation. Sometimes spending a little more on rent and being more centrally located might end up saving you a lot of time, and time is the most important currency we have. It could also save on gas as well if you move to a city where you need a car. In addition, more vibrant neighborhoods have many amenities and businesses within a short walk away.

When looking for accommodations, online groups, Facebook groups, and online ads can be a good place to start. However, not everyone in these groups may give sound advice, so be cautious.

Going through friends who might know someone who might know someone is often easier, even temporarily.

Sometimes, living close to work can be a good start. My advice, avoid signing long leases unless you are sure of yourself. Negotiate a shorter lease or month-to-month if possible, or if your situation allows for it, find a room to rent in a house or apartment – it's that simple.

If you don't know anyone like I did when I first landed, I chose to live in the middle of the action. Easier access to work, and considering I didn't have a car, I could walk to the grocery store. But the price tag of my apartment was a bit of a shock, and to secure the lease, given my non-existent credit history, I had to dig deep in my pockets. The management asked for a two-month rent deposit plus two months' rent in advance. Yes, you did the math correctly—four times the rent to have a roof over my head. I later met people who sometimes had to pay six months upfront or more. Retrospectively, here's what I would do now if I could go back in time. I'd look online on Roommates.com or SpareRoom.com for a room to rent in a roommate-type configuration or co-living arrangement for their more flexible lease options.

Even though I enjoyed having my own place, it did put unnecessary financial stress on my shoulders while starting out, given that you never know how your start will be. And sharing would have allowed me to meet new people as well. And I hear what you're thinking, "Sure, but living with people isn't always ideal," but even for just a few months, it can actually give you the time you need to land on your feet without adding more pressure on yourself and your finances.

a) Renting

When renting a place, make sure to ask about the deposit, pet policies, and extra fees, as well as whether or not any additional charges like utilities (water, gas, electricity, and sewage) are included in the rent. Extra sets of keys, gate keys, and last but not least, a parking space are other essential elements to be on the lookout for, as they are not always included and can be a considerable added cost.

Websites like Zillow, Trulia, or Apartments.com are good resources to start looking for accommodations to rent or buy.

Finding a place to live can be challenging, but with a little research and patience, you can find the perfect pad for you and your family (including your furry friends).

Quick Tips

1. Research the Neighborhoods: Consider factors such as safety, accessibility to public transportation, proximity to shops and restaurants, and the availability of amenities like parks and gyms. This will help you narrow down your options and focus on neighborhoods that fit your needs.

2. Check Reviews and Ratings: When searching for accommodations online, be sure to check out reviews and ratings of the property and the landlord or property manager. This will give you a good idea of what to expect and help you avoid any potential issues.

3. Consider Short-Term Rentals: If you are only planning to stay in a city for a short period, consider short-term rentals like Airbnb, VRBO, or misterb&b. These can often be a better deal than traditional long-term rentals and offer more flexibility, and they come furnished.

4. Ask for Referrals: Don't be afraid to ask friends, family, or colleagues if they know of any available rental properties. They may be able to refer you to a landlord or property manager who has a vacancy that fits your needs.

5. Negotiate Your Rent: Once you have found a property that you are interested in, don't be afraid to negotiate your rent. Landlords may be willing to offer discounts or other incentives if you sign a longer lease or pay rent in advance.

Be Prepared to Pay Deposits and Fees: When renting a property, you will typically be required to pay a security deposit, which can range from one to three months' rent. You may also be required to pay application fees, credit check fees, and other administrative costs. Now, when you leave your place, beware of cleaning fees you may be charged that will be deducted from the deposit the landlord must return to you. So when signing, ask about cleaning fees and anything else that could nibble parts of your deposit away.

Helpful Websites

- https://www.zillow.com/
- https://www.trulia.com/
- https://www.apartments.com/
- https://www.airbnb.com/
- https://www.vrbo.com/
- https://www.misterbandb.com/
- https://www.rent.com/
- https://hotpads.com/

Here are some popular websites where you can find roommates or co-living options:

- www.roommates.com
  A platform specifically designed for finding roommates. You can create a profile, search for compatible roommates based on various criteria, and connect with potential matches.

- www.roomster.com
  Roomster is a platform that helps you find roommates and shared accommodations. It offers a user-friendly interface and allows you to connect with potential roommates directly.

- www.spareroom.com
  SpareRoom is a popular website for finding roommates and shared housing. You can browse listings, set preferences, and communicate with potential roommates through the platform.

- www.padmapper.com
  PadMapper is a useful tool for finding apartments and roommates. It aggregates listings from various sources, including popular rental websites and classifieds.

- www.roomiapp.com
  Roomi is an app and website that connects potential roommates. It offers verified user profiles, messaging features, and search filters to help you find suitable living arrangements.

Remember to exercise caution and use your judgment when interacting with potential roommates online. It's essential to conduct thorough background checks, meet in person, and discuss expectations and compatibility before making any housing decisions.

And always read the fine print and ask questions before signing a lease or handing over any money.

b) Buying

When buying property in the United States, there are several factors to consider for foreigners, green card holders, and US citizens. Income and credit score play a vital role in securing a mortgage loan.

For US citizens and green card holders, having a stable income and a good credit score is crucial to securing favorable mortgage terms. Lenders assess these factors to determine the borrower's ability to repay the loan. A higher income and a solid credit score improve the chances of qualifying for more substantial loan amounts and better interest rates. Aiming for a 20% down payment will avoid having to take out a mortgage insurance plan on top of everything else.

If you're short on funds, FHA loans are here to save the day! FHA, or Federal Housing Administration, loans are a popular option for first-time homebuyers and those with limited down payment savings. These loans offer a fantastic opportunity to enter the housing market with a lower down payment requirement, making homeownership more accessible. Plus, the FHA's flexible guidelines and credit score leniency make it more likely to qualify, even if you don't have a flawless credit history. So say goodbye to hefty down payments and hello to the keys to your very own home with the help of an FHA loan, and make your homeownership dreams a reality!

Foreigners who are not US citizens or green card holders, especially those new to the country, often face more challenges when applying for a mortgage loan. Consequently, some foreign buyers decide to purchase properties with cash, eliminating the need to navigate the complex loan approval process and income verification. Before purchasing cash, ensure you have enough funds to cover all additional costs, typically called "closing costs."

Regardless of citizenship status, all buyers should seek guidance from real estate professionals who can also assist international buyers. These experts can provide valuable insights into the local market, legal requirements, and tax implications. Working with them streamlines the purchasing process and ensures compliance with relevant regulations.

Closing Costs

Below are some of the common closing costs:

1. Lender Fees: These are charges imposed by the mortgage lender and can include loan origination fees, appraisal fees, credit report fees, and underwriting fees.

2. Title and Escrow Fees: These costs are associated with the transfer of the property's title and the escrow services provided. They may include title search fees, title insurance premiums, escrow fees, and recording fees.

3. Government Taxes and Fees: This category includes taxes and fees imposed by local and state governments. Examples include property transfer taxes, documentary stamp taxes, and recording fees.

4. Attorney or Closing Agent Fees: Hiring an attorney or a closing agent to facilitate the transaction can incur additional costs. They may charge fees for preparing documents, reviewing contracts, and overseeing the closing process.

5. Home Inspection Fees: Conducting a professional inspection of the property is often recommended to identify any potential issues. The buyer is usually responsible for the cost of the inspection.

6. Homeowners Association (HOA) Fees: If the property is part of a homeowners association, there may be fees associated with membership, transfer of ownership, or obtaining HOA documents.

7. Property Insurance: Buyers are generally required to obtain homeowners insurance, and this cost may be paid at closing.

8. Prepaid Expenses: Some costs, such as property taxes, prepaid interest, and homeowner's insurance premiums, may be collected upfront and held in an escrow account by the lender.

In summary, collaborating with professionals experienced in assisting international buyers enhances the overall experience and helps navigate potential challenges.

Remember, it's always recommended to consult a qualified real estate professional or financial advisor for personalized advice and guidance when buying property. For all of these reasons, renting can help you build some credit history, establish yourself professionally, and give you time to decide where to buy.

Helpful Websites

Here are two websites that provide information about FHA loans and mortgages in America:

- Official FHA Website:

    https://www.hud.gov/program_offices/housing/fhahistory

    The official website of the Federal Housing Administration (FHA) provides comprehensive information about FHA loans, eligibility requirements, loan programs, and other resources for homebuyers. You can find detailed guidelines, calculators, and frequently asked questions to help you understand the ins and outs of FHA loans.

- Consumer Financial Protection Bureau (CFPB):

    https://www.consumerfinance.gov/

    The Consumer Financial Protection Bureau (CFPB) is a government agency that provides helpful resources to educate consumers about mortgages, including understanding mortgage terms, shopping for a mortgage, and avoiding common pitfalls. Their website offers guides, articles, and interactive tools to help you navigate the mortgage process.

These websites should provide enough valuable insights and resources to better understand FHA loans and mortgages in America. Remember to explore the official FHA website for specific details on FHA loan programs and the CFPB website for broader information on mortgages and consumer protections.

Chapter 6

SCHOOLS

Education Avenue

Navigating the complex world of school choices can feel like wandering through a labyrinth. It's a topic that could fill an entire book! Don't worry, I won't leave you in the dark. Allow me to shed some light and offer a few pointers to guide you toward making the perfect decision for yourself and your loved ones.

There are various avenues to explore when it comes to school options:

Public schools

Public schools are government-funded institutions that provide free education to students within a given district.

They offer comprehensive academic programs that adhere to standardized curricula established by educational authorities. Public schools strive to provide equal access to education for all students and frequently have a diverse student body, while also striving to provide a well-rounded education as well as a variety of extracurricular activities and access to a variety of support services.

Charter schools

Charter schools are innovative and autonomous public schools that operate under a charter (a "contract"), allowing them greater flexibility in curriculum, teaching methods, and administration. These schools often have a unique educational focus, offering specialized programs and alternative approaches to traditional public schooling. With a commitment to academic excellence and community engagement, charter schools provide students with diverse educational opportunities tailored to their individual needs. Also, if the public school in your district is too crowded, this can be an alternative.

While it is true that some charter schools are operated by private organizations or entities, keep in mind that not all charter schools are run as a business. Charter schools can be operated by a variety of entities, including nonprofit organizations, community groups, universities, or even public school districts. The specific management and governance structure of a charter school can vary depending on state laws and regulations. Some charter schools may have more autonomy in decision-making and administration compared to traditional public schools, but their primary focus is still on providing quality education to students rather than profit generation. It's crucial to research the specific policies and practices of the charter school you're considering to get a complete picture of how they operate.

Private schools

Private schools are educational institutions that operate independently and are funded through tuition fees and private sources. With smaller class sizes and more intimate learning environments, private schools often prioritize individualized attention and offer a range of academic programs, extracurricular activities, and specialized resources. Private schools may adhere to particular philosophies, religious affiliations, or unique educational approaches, providing families with a choice for an education tailored to their values and aspirations. Note that the level of education in private schools differs from one school to another and from one state to another.

Homeschooling

Homeschooling, a form of education conducted at home, offers the freedom and flexibility to design a personalized learning experience. Parents or guardians become the primary educators, tailoring the curriculum to their child's strengths, interests, and learning styles. Homeschooling fosters a nurturing environment that promotes one-on-one instruction, customized educational materials, and the ability to create a flexible schedule. It allows families to embrace a hands-on, experiential approach to education, nurturing a love of learning and individualized growth.

The specific steps for homeschooling may vary depending on your location and local regulations.

Since this one may be a bit tricky, let's take the example of Los Angeles for general steps to consider when homeschooling:

1. Familiarize yourself with California homeschooling laws: Research the homeschooling laws and regulations specific to California and Los Angeles County. In California, homeschooling is legally recognized as a private school, so you will need to comply with the relevant laws and regulations.

2. File a Private School Affidavit (PSA): As a homeschooling parent in California, you will need to file a PSA with the California Department of Education (CDE) between October 1 and October 15 each year. This is a simple form that registers your homeschool as a private school. The CDE website provides guidance and resources for filing the PSA.

3. Choose a homeschooling curriculum: Select a curriculum or educational approach that aligns with your child's learning needs and educational goals. California does not prescribe a specific curriculum, allowing flexibility in choosing materials and resources.

4. Keep attendance records: Maintain accurate attendance records for each school day. California requires 180 days of instruction per school year.

5. Cover required subjects: California law requires that homeschools cover the following subjects: English,

mathematics, social sciences, science, fine arts, health, and physical education. Ensure that your curriculum includes these subjects.

6. Keep records of your child's progress. Document your child's academic progress, including samples of their work, grades, and assessments. This helps demonstrate that your child is receiving an appropriate education.

7. Participate in standardized testing or assessments: California law requires students in certain grades to participate in standardized testing or assessments. Familiarize yourself with the specific requirements and ensure compliance.

8. Consider joining a homeschooling support group. Connecting with local homeschooling support groups or organizations can provide valuable resources, networking opportunities, and support from experienced homeschooling parents.

9. Stay informed and up-to-date: Stay informed about any changes in homeschooling laws or regulations in California. Regularly check the California Department of Education website and join relevant homeschooling associations or online forums to stay updated.

It's important to note that these steps are a general guide, and it is advisable to consult with local homeschooling organizations, support groups, or legal professionals in Los Angeles for specific guidance and compliance with local regulations.

The California Department of Education (CDE) website:

https://www.cde.ca.gov/

This website is a great resource for information on homeschooling in California, including guidelines, forms, and other relevant resources. You can navigate through the website to find specific information related to homeschooling in Los Angeles and the state of California.

In general, the homeschooling curriculum is designed to provide a comprehensive and personalized education tailored to the unique needs and circumstances of each child.

A homeschooling curriculum typically includes subjects such as mathematics, language arts (reading, writing, and grammar), science, social studies, history, foreign languages, the arts, physical education, and other elective subjects. The curriculum may consist of textbooks, workbooks, online courses, educational websites, educational software, hands-on materials, and other resources.

Homeschooling families have the flexibility to choose from a wide range of curriculum options available on the market. Some families prefer pre-packaged curriculum sets that provide a comprehensive and structured approach to education, while others opt for a more eclectic approach, combining various materials from different publishers and sources to create a customized curriculum.

Homeschooling parents need to consider their child's learning style, interests, strengths, and weaknesses when selecting a homeschool curriculum. The curriculum should align with the educational goals of the family and provide a well-rounded education that meets state requirements (if applicable). Additionally, homeschooling parents can adapt, modify, or supplement the curriculum as needed to suit their child's learning pace.

Helpful Websites about Homeschooling

Here are some valuable information, resources, and support for homeschooling families:

1. Home School Legal Defense Association (HSLDA): www.hslda.org

    HSLDA offers legal support and resources for homeschooling families. They provide information on state homeschooling laws, advocacy, curriculum guidance, and various homeschooling resources.

2. The Homeschool Mom: www.thehomeschoolmom.com

    The Homeschool Mom is a comprehensive website offering curriculum reviews, educational resources, free printables, articles, and a community forum for homeschooling parents to connect and support one another.

3. Home Educators Association of Virginia (HEAV): www.heav.org

    While focused on homeschooling in Virginia, the HEAV website provides a wealth of resources, including articles, curriculum reviews, legal information, and helpful tools that can be applied to homeschoolers nationwide.

4. Simply Charlotte Mason: www.simplycharlottemason.com

    This website is dedicated to the Charlotte Mason educational approach, offering guidance, curriculum resources, and practical tips for implementing the Charlotte Mason method in homeschooling.

5. Time4Learning: www.time4learning.com

   Time4Learning is an online curriculum provider that offers interactive, multimedia-based courses for homeschooling students from pre-K to high school. They cover various subjects and provide a structured learning experience.

6. Khan Academy: www.khanacademy.org

   Khan Academy is a popular educational website offering a wide range of video lessons, exercises, and practice quizzes across numerous subjects. It can be a valuable supplemental resource for homeschooling families.

Community Colleges

Community colleges, also known as junior colleges or technical colleges, typically offer two-year associate degree programs. They primarily serve local communities and provide accessible and affordable higher education options. Community colleges often offer vocational and technical programs as well as transferable credits that allow students to continue their education at a four-year college or university. They tend to have smaller class sizes and a focus on practical skills and workforce preparation.

Colleges

In the United States, "college" is often used interchangeably with "university," but it can also refer to smaller, independent institutions that offer undergraduate programs. These colleges typically grant bachelor's degrees and may specialize in specific fields such as liberal arts, sciences, business, or fine arts. Colleges can be public or private, and while they offer a range of programs, they tend to have a more limited scope compared to universities.

Universities

Universities are institutions of higher education that offer a wide array of undergraduate and graduate programs across diverse fields of study. They are centers of knowledge, research, and academic exploration. Universities provide students with the opportunity to deepen their knowledge, develop critical thinking skills, and pursue specialized areas of interest. They often foster a vibrant campus life, including student organizations, cultural events, and access to extensive resources such as libraries, laboratories, and expert faculty. Universities serve as hubs for intellectual growth, career development, and the pursuit of higher learning.

It's important to note that terminology and distinctions can vary between different countries and regions, so it's always a good idea to research specific institutions to understand their unique offerings and characteristics.

Student Loans and Financial Aid

Loans for college and financial aid play a key part in helping students afford higher education. Here is some information about loans for college and how financial aid works for students:

1. Federal Student Loans: The U.S. Department of Education offers federal student loans, which typically have lower interest rates and more favorable repayment terms compared to private loans. There are two main types of federal student loans: direct subsidized loans (based on financial need) and direct unsubsidized loans (not based on financial need). These loans must be repaid after graduation or when the student drops below half-time enrollment.

2. Private Student Loans: Banks, credit unions, and other financial institutions offer private student loans. They can be an option when additional funds are needed beyond what federal student loans and other financial aid cover. Private student loans often require a credit check and may have higher interest rates compared to federal loans.

3. Financial Aid: Financial aid refers to a variety of grants, scholarships, work-study programs, and loans that help students cover the cost of education. Financial aid is awarded based on factors such as financial need, academic merit, and other criteria set by the institution or external organizations. To apply for financial aid, students must complete the Free Application for Federal Student Aid (FAFSA) or, in some cases, additional institutional aid applications.

4. FAFSA: The FAFSA is a crucial step in applying for federal and some state financial aid programs. It collects information about a student's family income, assets, and other factors to determine eligibility for need-based aid. The FAFSA is available online, and students should submit it as early as possible to meet deadlines and maximize their financial aid opportunities.

5. Expected Family Contribution (EFC): The EFC is a number calculated based on the information provided on the FAFSA. It represents the amount the student and their family are expected to contribute toward their education. The EFC helps determine the student's eligibility for need-based financial aid programs.

6. Grants and scholarships are forms of financial aid that do not require repayment. They can be awarded by the federal government, state governments, colleges, universities, or private organizations. Grants and scholarships are typically awarded based on financial need, academic achievements, talents, or other specific criteria.

7. Work-Study Programs: Work-study programs provide students with part-time job opportunities, often on campus, to earn money to help cover their educational expenses. Work-study positions are typically need-based and allow students to gain work experience while earning money for their education.

Students and their families need to research the various types of loans and financial aid available, as well as have a firm understanding of the application processes and deadlines. Each college or university may have its own policies and requirements regarding financial aid, so it's essential to consult with the school's financial aid office for specific information and guidance. Additionally, many resources are available online, such as the official FAFSA website https://studentaid.gov/h/apply-for-aid/fafsa, to help navigate the financial aid process.

Higher education in the US can come with a hefty price tag. I've got some valuable tips to help you start your education for free. Check out these websites; they are excellent online resources that won't cost you a dime, or very little. Take advantage of these online sources of knowledge and make your educational journey more affordable. Start exploring them today and unlock a world of learning opportunities.

- Free lecture notes, exams, and videos from MIT: https://ocw.mit.edu/

- Free online courses from Harvard University: https://www.edx.org/school/harvardx

- Simply input your field of interest, and the platform will curate a list of courses for you. While you can enjoy a few queries free of charge, it offers a monthly membership at an affordable rate of only $10 per month: https://www.tutorai.me/

Quick Tips

1. Research the school options in your area: Depending on where you live, you may have a variety of school options available to you. Take some time to research the different types of schools, including public, private, and charter schools, as well as homeschooling options.

2. Consider the curriculum: Different schools may offer different curriculums, so it's important to consider what kind of education you want your child to receive. Some schools may focus on STEM subjects, while others may focus more on the arts or humanities.

3. Look into the school's reputation: Research the reputation of the schools you're considering, as well as their rankings and reviews. Websites like Greatschools.org can provide helpful information on school ratings and reviews.

4. Visit the schools: Once you've narrowed down your options, visit the schools in person to get a better sense of their atmosphere and to meet with teachers and administrators.

5. Understand the costs: Private schools can be expensive, so make sure you understand the costs associated with each school option. Public schools are typically free, but you may need to pay for supplies, uniforms, or other expenses.

Helpful Websites

- https://www.greatschools.org
  Provides ratings and reviews of schools across the US, as well as information on their academic performance, diversity, and more.

- https://nces.ed.gov
  National Center for Education Statistics: Provides data and statistics on US schools and universities, including graduation rates, test scores, and more.

- https://www.usnews.com/education
  U.S. News & World Report Education Rankings: Provides rankings of US universities and colleges based on factors like academic quality, graduation rates, and student outcomes.

- https://www.collegeboard.org
  College Board: Provides information on college admissions, including how to choose a college, how to apply, and how to pay for college.

In the exciting world of education, schools offer a rainbow of possibilities. Whether you're considering charter schools, homeschooling, private schools, public schools, or the vast realm of colleges and universities, remember this: school's in session, and you hold the key to unlocking a world of knowledge and opportunity. So explore, and let your or your child's educational adventure begin! And do not forget to ask all the questions crossing your mind.

CHAPTER 7

HEALTH INSURANCE

Navigating the Health Insurance Maze

Welcome to the wild world of health insurance in the United States! It's a dimension where acronyms, fine print, and confusing terminology reign supreme. So buckle up, grab a pen, and let's embark on this adventure together.

Now, I know what you're thinking. Health insurance? Isn't that supposed to make things easier? Well, in theory, yes. But in practice, it often feels like navigating a labyrinth filled with insurance jargon, mind-boggling deductibles, and a seemingly endless parade of paperwork. It's like trying to decipher an ancient code while juggling flaming torches.

First things first, let's address the elephant in the room: the cost. Yes, health insurance in the US can be expensive. It's like shopping for a designer handbag, except instead of just breaking the bank, you're potentially breaking your entire financial future. Not to worry, there are ways to find affordable options without sacrificing your sanity.

Next, we need to tackle the beast known as coverage. Insurance plans come in all shapes and sizes, which is why it is crucial to understand what your plan covers and what it doesn't to avoid any unexpected surprise.

Let's not forget about the joyous process of enrolling in a health insurance plan. We'll dive into the enrollment process, demystify the terminology, and provide you with the tools to make an informed decision. You'll be strutting into that doctor's office like a well-prepared healthcare guru in no time.

So, let's get started.

Cost

It's no secret that the cost of health insurance in the United States can be a significant financial consideration. Like a coin with two sides, health insurance premiums and out-of-pocket expenses play a crucial role in determining the overall cost. Premiums are the monthly payments you make to maintain your insurance coverage, while out-of-pocket expenses encompass deductibles, copayments, and coinsurance. It's important to strike a balance between a premium that fits your budget and coverage that meets your healthcare needs. However, don't let the cost deter you from obtaining insurance, as being uninsured can lead to hefty medical bills in the event of an unexpected illness or injury. Remember, health insurance is a wise investment for your well-being and peace of mind. In our journey together, we'll explore strategies to navigate the financial aspects, find affordable options, and make informed decisions about your coverage while keeping your budget in mind.

Finding affordable health insurance options can be a daunting task, but there are strategies to help you navigate the complex landscape and find coverage that fits your budget. Here are some steps to consider:

1. Assess Your Needs: Start by understanding your healthcare needs. Consider factors such as your age, medical history, and any specific treatments or medications you require. This will help you determine the level of coverage you need without overpaying for unnecessary services.

2. Explore Marketplace Plans: In the US, the Health Insurance Marketplace is a valuable resource where you can compare and purchase health insurance plans. These plans are designed to meet certain coverage standards and often offer subsidies based on your income level. You can visit the official Marketplace website or use private websites that aggregate plans for easier comparison.

3. Research Medicaid and CHIP: If you have limited income, you may qualify for Medicaid or the Children's Health Insurance Program (CHIP). These government-funded programs provide low-cost or free health coverage to eligible individuals and families. Check the eligibility criteria in your state and consider applying if you meet the requirements.

4. Consider Catastrophic Plans: Catastrophic health insurance plans are designed to provide coverage for major medical events and emergencies. They typically

have lower premiums but higher deductibles. If you're generally healthy and don't require frequent medical care, a catastrophic plan can be a more affordable option.

5. Look into Short-Term Plans: Short-term health insurance plans offer temporary coverage for a specific period, usually up to a year. While they may have limitations in coverage, they can provide a cost-effective solution if you're in between jobs or waiting for another insurance option to kick in.

6. Check with Professional Associations: Some professional or trade associations offer group health insurance plans for their members. These plans can often provide more affordable coverage due to group purchasing power. If you're part of an association, inquire about any health insurance options available to you.

7. Seek Assistance from Insurance Brokers: Insurance brokers are professionals who can help you navigate the insurance market and find the most suitable and affordable plans for your needs. They have in-depth knowledge of different insurance options and can guide you through the process.

Remember, it is crucial to carefully review the terms and coverage details of any health insurance plan you're considering. Pay attention to deductibles, copayments, and network restrictions to ensure the plan aligns with your healthcare needs and financial situation. By being proactive, researching your options, and seeking assistance when needed, you can increase your chances of finding affordable health insurance that provides the coverage you need.

Enrolling

The enrollment period for health insurance in the United States typically takes place once a year. The specific dates can vary depending on the year and the type of health insurance plan you are considering. However, the most common enrollment period for individual health insurance plans is from November 1st to December 15th. This period is applicable for coverage that would start on January 1st of the following year. It's important to note that these dates are subject to change, so it's always a good idea to check with the official health insurance marketplace or the specific insurance provider for the most up-to-date information regarding the enrollment period.

Enrolling in a health insurance plan in the United States is an essential step to ensuring access to necessary medical care. The process may vary depending on your circumstances, but there are generally a few common paths to enrollment. For individuals and families, the most common route is through the Health Insurance Marketplace, where you can explore different plans and choose the one that suits your needs. Open enrollment periods typically occur once a year, during which you can sign up for coverage or make changes to your existing plan. Outside of the open enrollment period, you may still be able to enroll if you qualify for a special enrollment period, triggered by certain life events such as getting married, having a baby, or losing job-based coverage.

It's important to note that some individuals may be eligible for public insurance programs like Medicaid or the Children's Health Insurance Program (CHIP), which have their own enrollment processes. To enroll, you'll need to provide personal information, such as proof of identity and income, and carefully follow the instructions provided. Be aware of enrollment deadlines and take proactive steps to ensure you and your loved ones have the necessary coverage in place.

Medicaid vs. Medicare

Medicaid and Medicare are two distinct healthcare programs in the United States, each serving different populations. Medicaid is a joint federal and state program designed to provide health coverage for low-income individuals and families. It is primarily administered by the states and offers a range of comprehensive healthcare services to eligible individuals, including doctor visits, hospital stays, prescription drugs, and preventive care. The eligibility criteria and coverage options can vary from state to state.

On the other hand, Medicare is a federal health insurance program primarily for people aged 65 and older, as well as individuals with certain disabilities or end-stage renal disease. It consists of different parts, including Part A (hospital insurance), Part B (medical insurance), Part C (Medicare Advantage plans), and Part D (prescription drug coverage). Medicare is administered by the federal government and provides a wide range of healthcare services and coverage options tailored to the specific needs of eligible individuals.

In summary, Medicaid is a state-based program aimed at providing health coverage to low-income individuals, while Medicare is a federal program that primarily serves older adults and individuals with disabilities. Understanding the distinction between the two programs is essential for individuals seeking appropriate healthcare coverage based on their specific circumstances and eligibility criteria.

Example:

Please note that in California, the state's Medicaid program is called Medi-Cal. It follows the guidelines and regulations set by the federal Medicaid program but is administered by the California Department of Health Care Services (DHCS).

So, when discussing Medicaid in California, the term "Medi-Cal" is commonly used.

Insurance Coverage

Understanding health insurance coverage in the United States can be a puzzle, but let's break it down into manageable pieces. "Coverage" refers to the range of medical services and treatments that your health insurance plan will pay for.

Typically, insurance plans cover a variety of services, including doctor visits, hospital stays, prescription medications, preventive care, and more. However, the extent of coverage can vary depending on the specific plan you choose. It's important to carefully review the plan's benefits and limitations, such as deductibles, copayments, and coinsurance, to grasp how much you'll be responsible for paying out of pocket. Additionally, many insurance plans have a network of healthcare providers, and it's important to check if your preferred doctors and hospitals are "in-network" to ensure the highest level of coverage. By understanding the basics of coverage and doing your research, you can make informed decisions when selecting a health insurance plan that aligns with your healthcare needs.

HMO vs. PPO

HMO, PPO, here we go! Let's unravel the health plan show. In this battle of acronyms, we'll discover the differences between them, one after another.

HMO (Health Maintenance Organization):

- HMOs operate through a network of healthcare providers and facilities.
- You choose a primary care physician (PCP) who manages your healthcare.
- Referrals from your PCP are usually required to see specialists.
- Out-of-network care is usually not covered, except in emergencies.
- HMOs often have lower premiums and out-of-pocket costs.
- They may require you to select healthcare providers from their network.

PPO (Preferred Provider Organization):

- PPOs offer more flexibility and choice to healthcare providers.

- You can see specialists without needing a referral from a primary care physician.

- PPOs cover both in-network and out-of-network care, although at different rates.

- Out-of-network care typically has higher costs and may require meeting a deductible.

- PPOs generally have higher premiums compared to HMOs.

- You have the freedom to see any healthcare provider, but using in-network providers results in greater cost savings.

When deciding between HMO and PPO plans, consider factors such as your healthcare needs, preferred providers, and financial considerations. HMOs may be a better fit if you prefer a coordinated approach with lower costs, while PPOs offer more flexibility at a higher price point. Assessing your circumstances and priorities will help you make an informed decision about the most suitable health insurance plan for you.

Quick Tips

1. Research your options: There are quite a few types of health insurance plans available, including employer-sponsored plans, individual plans, and government-sponsored plans, like Medicaid and Medicare. Take some time to research the different types of plans and which ones you may be eligible for.

2. Consider your needs: Evaluate your healthcare needs, such as prescription medications, regular doctor visits, and specialist care. Look for a plan that covers the services you need and has a network of providers in your area.

3. Compare plans: Once you know what you need, compare plans from different insurance providers. Look at the premiums, deductibles, and out-of-pocket costs for each plan, as well as any limitations on coverage or provider networks.

4. Check for subsidies: Depending on your income and family size, you may be eligible for assistance to help pay for health insurance premiums. Check with your state's health insurance marketplace or healthcare.gov to see if you qualify.

5. Consider a broker: If you're having trouble finding a plan that meets your needs and budget, consider working with a health insurance broker. Brokers can help you compare plans and find the best fit for your situation.

6. Read the fine print: Before signing up for a health insurance plan, make sure you understand the details of the coverage, including any limitations or exclusions. Pay attention to the network of providers and any out-of-pocket costs you're responsible for.

7. Stay informed: Keep track of any changes to your health insurance policy, such as changes in coverage or pricing. Make sure you understand how to use your plan, such as how to find a provider or submit a claim.

Helpful Websites

- https://www.healthcare.gov
  The official health insurance marketplace for the United States, where you can compare plans and enroll in coverage.

- https://www.ehealthinsurance.com
  A website that allows you to compare health insurance plans from multiple providers and get quotes.

- https://www.healthsherpa.com
  A website that helps you find and enroll in health insurance plans, including Medicaid and Medicare.

Your state's health insurance marketplace: Most states have their own health insurance marketplace where you can compare plans and enroll in coverage.

- https://www.medicaid.gov/
- https://www.medicare.gov/
- https://www.medi-cal.ca.gov/
- https://www.dhcs.ca.gov/
- https://www.insurekidsnow.gov/

  The website for the Children's Health Insurance Program (CHIP) varies depending on the state you reside in. Each state operates its own CHIP program, even though it receives federal funding. To find the specific website for CHIP in your state, you can use the InsureKidsNow.

gov website, which provides a directory of state-specific programs.

You can visit the InsureKidsNow.gov website and select your state from the drop-down menu or map on the homepage. It will redirect you to the appropriate website for your state's CHIP program, where you can find detailed information, eligibility criteria, enrollment processes, and other resources related to children's health insurance.

Remember, finding the right health insurance plan can take time and effort, but it's an important step in protecting your health and financial well-being. Don't rush into a decision, and make sure you understand the details of your coverage before you sign up.

CHAPTER 8

BUYING OR LEASING A CAR

On the Road to Automotive Bliss

Ah, the freedom of the open road! There's nothing like getting behind the wheel of your very own car and hitting the pavement. But before you can feel that rush, you'll have to think about how to first acquire your ride.

Buying a car is a big decision that ultimately comes down to your budget. If you're in the market for a brand-new car, hit up a dealership and do some research beforehand. This is America, and everything is negotiable - don't be afraid to haggle that price down until it's the best deal for you.

Leasing a car is another option, but it requires jumping through a few extra hoops like providing a social security number and sometimes even a guarantor if you're new in the country. It's up to you to decide if it's worth the hassle.

For those who want to save a little cash, buying a used car is also a good option. However, it can be a bit of a gamble as you never know what repairs may be needed down the road. If you're not a car expert (and let's be real, who is?), try to have it checked by a mechanic before the title transfer and any exchange of money.

And consider the cost of fixing your ride. European cars are significantly more expensive to fix than American or Asian cars. I learned that firsthand when I purchased a used German convertible. Oh, how fun it was driving until the problems started flooding in and I had to sell it for a huge loss and get a Honda, which has been one of the best investments I ever made in terms of cars (if cars could even be considered as such). At the time, I didn't know anyone or a mechanic, and when I tell you to not be shy and ask questions, it is because I made those mistakes myself, and it did cost quite a lot. So before buying any used car, find a mechanic, ask anyone, search for recommendations online, join Facebook groups, and make a deal with the potential seller to have the car checked before buying it. Usually, if no issue is hidden from you, the seller will agree to that. After all, good business is good business, right?

Of course, with car ownership comes the responsibility of insurance and registration. If you're financing a car, you'll need full coverage insurance. And if you're a new driver, prepare for higher insurance costs. If you buy your car outright, you're only required to get liability insurance, but I recommend getting full coverage just in case.

Research online for the best insurance deals as prices can vary depending on your location. And don't forget about the American Automobile Association, aka AAA. For a small membership fee, you can get access to their DMV services like car registration, and car insurance. Plus, their roadside assistance service is top-notch.

Quick Tips

1. Research prices online:

   Before visiting a dealership, research prices online to get an idea of the car you want. Websites such as Kelley Blue Book, Edmunds, and TrueCar can provide you with information on the average price of the car you're interested in.

2. Negotiate the price:

   Don't be afraid to negotiate the price of a car with a dealer. Be assertive and let them know what you're willing to pay. You may be able to negotiate a lower price or get some additional features added to the car.

3. Consider leasing:

   Leasing a car can be a good option if you don't want to commit to buying a car outright or can't afford the monthly payments. However, keep in mind that leasing can have restrictions on mileage and excessive wear and tear.

4. Check out used cars:

   Used cars can be a great option if you're looking for a cheaper alternative. However, be sure to get a vehicle history report and have a mechanic inspect the car before making a purchase.

5. Get a AAA membership:

   AAA (pronounced "Triple-A") offers services for car owners, including roadside assistance, insurance, and DMV services. Membership can be a good investment if you are looking for peace of mind and convenience.

Helpful Websites

- Kelley Blue Book: www.kbb.com
- Edmunds: www.edmunds.com
- TrueCar: www.truecar.com
- Carfax: www.carfax.com
- AAA: www.aaa.com

Car Insurance

When buying a car, factor in the cost of insurance. Shop around for the best rates and consider getting quotes from multiple insurance providers.

If you're new to shopping for car insurance in the US, here are some valuable tips to help you navigate the process effectively:

- Understand your coverage needs: Determine the level of coverage you require based on your state's minimum requirements and your circumstances. Consider factors such as your car's value, your driving habits, and any additional coverage you may need, like comprehensive or collision insurance.

- Research insurance companies: Search for reliable companies with top-notch customer support and good financial standing. Some major insurance companies in the US include State Farm, Geico, Progressive, Allstate, Farmers Insurance, Liberty Mutual, Nationwide, American Family Insurance, and Travelers Insurance. Check online reviews to gain insights into their reputation and claims process. Consider both national and local insurers to explore a wide range of options.

- Gather quotes from multiple insurers. Obtain quotes from several companies to compare prices and coverage options. You can use online comparison websites or contact insurance agents directly. Be prepared to provide accurate and consistent information to get the most accurate quotes.

- Evaluate coverage and deductibles: compare the coverage limits, deductibles, and optional features offered by different insurers. Assess how these factors align with your needs and budget. Remember, a lower premium may come with higher deductibles, so find the right balance for your financial situation.

- Consider discounts and savings: ask about discounts such as safe driver discounts, multi-policy discounts (bundling auto and home insurance), good student discounts, and anti-theft device discounts. Take advantage of any savings opportunities that apply to you.

- Review the policy terms and conditions: Carefully read and understand the terms and conditions of each policy. Pay attention to exclusions, limitations, and any additional fees or penalties. Seek clarification from the insurance company or agent if you have any doubts or questions.

- Don't focus solely on price. While cost is a factor, don't base your decision solely on price. Consider the overall value of the coverage, the customer service reputation, and the insurer's responsiveness when handling claims.

- Maintain a good driving record: Practice safe driving habits to maintain a clean driving record. Good driving history can lead to lower insurance premiums over time.

- Seek advice from professionals: If you're unsure about any aspect of car insurance, consider consulting with an independent insurance agent who can provide guidance and help you make an informed decision.

Remember, car insurance is an important protection, so take the time to research, ask friends where they get their insurance from, compare options, and choose the policy that best suits your needs and budget.

Helpful Websites

These websites can help you research and compare car insurance plans:

- The Zebra: www.thezebra.com
- Compare.com: www.compare.com
- Insurify: www.insurify.com

- NerdWallet: www.nerdwallet.com/insurance
- Policygenius: www.policygenius.com
- SmartFinancial: www.smartfinancial.com

Remember, buying or leasing a car is a big decision and requires careful consideration. Take your time and do your research before making a purchase.

Now that you have your wheels sorted, it's time to focus on landing the job of your dreams. But before you can start collecting paychecks, you need to craft a winning resume and stand out in a sea of applicants.

Chapter 9

RESUME & COVER LETTER

The Job Jungle: Resumes, LinkedIn, and Landing that Dream Job

Times are changing rapidly and, in the United States, having a solid LinkedIn profile is crucial.

Let's start by giving it some attention and making it shine. LinkedIn offers an array of job opportunities from numerous companies, making it an excellent place to kickstart your job search.

Resumes come in many different forms, depending on your field. Don't worry, though! You can find helpful guidelines online or through LinkedIn to assist you in creating a professional resume. Note that you don't have to include your full address or a headshot.

Creating a resume that catches the attention of potential employers can be challenging. It's like navigating a maze of keywords and phrasing. Consider seeking the assistance of a resume specialist who can help you present your skills and experience effectively.

If you have friends who can recommend you for a position in their company, it's a great advantage. The job market is highly competitive, and some individuals may have a head start due to their prior experience or connections. However, always believe in yourself and be aware of the difficulties of job hunting, particularly in competitive fields like entertainment.

Finding a job can be a real journey, but with the right tools, a positive mindset, and a sprinkle of self-confidence, you'll be well on your way to securing that dream job. Keep pushing forward, embrace the process, and let the world witness your talent. The stage is set, and it's time to make your grand entrance.

Quick Tips

1. Use online resources: Many websites offer free templates and advice on how to structure your resume and cover letter. Some of the popular ones include Indeed, Monster, and Glassdoor.
2. Tailor your resume: Customize your resume and cover letter for each job application. Highlight your relevant skills and experience that match the job description. This will increase your chances of getting noticed by the employer.

3. Use keywords: Many companies use Applicant Tracking Systems (ATS) to filter out resumes that do not meet certain criteria. To avoid being filtered out, make sure to use keywords from the job description in your resume and cover letter.

4. Keep it concise: Hiring managers and recruiters have limited time to review resumes. Keep your resume and cover letter concise and to the point. Limit your resume to one or two pages and your cover letter to one page.

5. Proofread: Make sure to proofread your resume and cover letter for spelling and grammatical errors. Ask a friend or mentor to review it as well.

6. Use LinkedIn: LinkedIn is a valuable tool for networking and job searching. Make sure to have a complete profile with a professional profile picture and headline. Join industry groups and connect with professionals in your field.

7. Consider hiring a professional: If you are struggling with your resume and cover letter, consider hiring a professional resume writer or career coach. They can provide personalized advice and help you create a resume and cover letter that stands out.

Helpful Websites

- Indeed Resume Tips:

    https://www.indeed.com/career-advice/resumes-cover-letters

- Monster Resume Center:

    https://www.monster.com/career-advice/resume-center

- Glassdoor Resume Guide:

    https://www.glassdoor.com/blog/guide/how-to-write-a-resume/

- Kickresume Resume Builder:

    https://www.kickresume.com/en/ai-resume-writer/

- The Muse Cover Letter Guide:

    https://www.themuse.com/advice/how-to-write-a-cover-letter-31-tips-you-need-to-know

Now that you know how to prepare the tools you need to get hired, you may be one of those ready for the exhilarating realm of starting your own business. Leave behind the traditional job hunt as we transition from crafting the perfect resume to unleashing your innovative ideas and carving your path. Get ready to ignite your entrepreneurial fire and embark on the thrilling journey of building your dreams from the ground up.

CHAPTER 10

STARTING A BUSINESS

Unleashing Your Entrepreneurial Spirit

Congratulations, my ambitious friends! You're about to embark on the thrilling journey of starting your own business. But hold your horses, because there are a few things you need to consider before diving in headfirst.

First and foremost, pick up that phone and give a ring to a Certified Practicing Accountant, also known as a CPA. Trust me, a CPA will be your saving grace in navigating the intricate world of business finances.

Now, let's talk about research. Don't be the daring entrepreneur who jumps into the business world without doing their homework. The costs of starting a business vary greatly depending on your state of residence. So roll up your sleeves and dig deep into the details.

You can't ignore taxes if you want your business to succeed, and to make matters more complex, tax requirements differ based on your area of expertise and business structure. That's where your friendly neighborhood CPA swoops in to save the day. Whether you choose to start an S Corp, C Corp, or LLC, they'll guide you through the maze and ensure you don't face any unnecessary tax troubles. Trust me on this, a reliable CPA is worth their weight in gold.

If you're looking to test the waters, consider starting as a sole proprietorship. As a sole proprietor, you have complete ownership of an unincorporated business. For a fee of $299, you can obtain an EIN (Employer Identification Number) from the IRS (this is tax deductible). While an EIN is not necessary if you don't plan on having employees, it offers advantages such as separating your personal and business finances. With an EIN, you can open a dedicated business account at a bank. If your business grows, you can later explore options like converting your EIN into an LLC, S Corp, and more.

And if you don't have a CPA in your contacts list, don't be afraid to connect with your network, ask for recommendations, and start making connections. You'll be grateful you did when the time comes to do your taxes.

While we're on the subject, let's not forget about choosing the right state for your business. It's like selecting the perfect stage for your performance. Each state has its own set of rules and advantages, so weigh your options carefully.

Starting a business is like stepping into uncharted territory, armed with your vision and determination. With the guidance of a CPA and careful consideration of state regulations, you're one step closer to making your entrepreneurial dreams a reality.

So let's put on our adventure hat and dive into the exciting world of business ownership. The sky's the limit, and success awaits those who dare to take it!

When to Open or Close a Business

Before opening a business, it is important to research and validate your business idea to ensure it is viable and has a target audience. Additionally, make sure to have a solid business plan in place and enough funding to cover initial costs.

When it comes to closing a business, it is important to do so in a timely and professional manner, with proper communication with customers, employees, and any other stakeholders. Seek the advice of a lawyer or accountant (CPA) to ensure all legal and financial obligations are met.

Helpful Websites

- Small Business Administration (SBA): Provides resources and guidance on starting, managing, and growing a small business, including business plan templates, funding options, and registration information.
- https://www.sba.gov/
- SCORE: A nonprofit organization that offers free mentoring, education, and resources for entrepreneurs. https://www.sba.gov/local-assistance/resource-partners/score-business-mentoring

- Entrepreneur: A business magazine and website that provides news, advice, and resources for small business owners and entrepreneurs. https://www.entrepreneur.com/
- IRS (Internal Service Revenue) – EIN application portal
- https://www.irs.gov/businesses/small-businesses-self-employed/apply-for-an-employer-identification-number-ein-online

Which Structure is Best

Choosing the proper business structure can impact taxes, liability, and ownership. Consulting with a CPA or lawyer can help determine which structure is best for your business.

Helpful Websites

- IRS Business Structures: Provides an overview of the different types of business structures. https://www.irs.gov/businesses/small-businesses-self-employed/business-structures
- Nolo: A website that provides legal information and resources for small business owners and entrepreneurs. https://www.nolo.com
- Incfile: An online platform that helps entrepreneurs and small business owners with business formation and compliance. https://www.incfile.com

Creating a Business Plan

A business plan is essential for starting and growing a successful business. It outlines your vision, goals, strategies, and financial projections. It might even help you in finding funding from lenders or investors. You can find business plan templates online or hire a professional to help you create one.

Funding Your Business

Starting a business requires capital, and there are many ways to fund your business. You can use your savings, borrow from friends and family, apply for a small business loan, or seek funding from investors or venture capitalists. Crowdfunding platforms like Kickstarter or Indiegogo can also be an option. Do your research and choose the funding method that works best for you and your business.

Registering Your Business

Once you've decided on a business structure and created a business plan, you'll need to register your business with your state and obtain any necessary licenses and permits. The Small Business Administration (SBA) website has a wealth of information on registering your business, as well as a list of state-specific resources.

Networking and Marketing

Building a network of contacts and marketing your business is essential for success. Attend networking events, join local business organizations, and use social media to connect with potential customers and partners. Consider hiring a marketing professional to help you develop a marketing plan and execute it effectively.

Continuing Education

Starting a business is an ongoing learning process, and it's important to stay up-to-date on industry trends and best practices. Attend workshops, webinars, and conferences, read business books and articles, and seek out guidance from experienced business owners.

Helpful Websites

- https://www.linkedin.com - a professional networking site where you can connect with other business owners and potential customers.

- https://www.udemy.com - an online learning platform with courses on various aspects of starting and growing a business.

If you think you have the stomach for this journey, there's a good chance that you will be successful. But be prepared and do your research first. Do not rush, and stay consistent. Fortune favors the brave!

CHAPTER 11

BUYING FOOD

Unveiling the Culinary Maze

You might be thinking, "Why on earth do I need advice on buying food? I've got this covered!" Well, hang on a second, because navigating the realm of food shopping in the United States requires a certain savoir-faire.

Sure, you can buy food anywhere, but buying *healthy* food, that's where knowledge comes into play. Brace yourself for an adventure filled with hidden sugars and other surprises.

Now, picture this: you're strolling through a well-known, fancy supermarket, grabbing what you think is the finest organic balsamic vinegar. But lo and behold, when you dress your salad, a wave of sweetness engulfs your taste buds. What sorcery is this? The label reveals the truth—it's laced with added sugar! Yes, I've experienced it myself on several occasions. As I closely monitor my sugar intake, I've become quite aware of this issue. In the food industry, sugar has a way of sneaking into products where it shouldn't be.

Like added sugar, you'll also find excessive sodium levels in many products that might surprise you. I once picked up a seemingly innocent organic can of soup, only to discover it contained enough salt to transform a freshwater oasis into a salt sea. But fear not, for I have a valuable tip to share:

Thou shalt always read the label!

I hear your collective groans. Who has the time to scrutinize every single label? But trust me, this time investment is worth it. Once you've discovered your go-to products and the trustworthy havens where they reside, the label-reading ritual will become second nature. Embrace your inner Sherlock Holmes of food choices!

Food restrictions and dietary considerations are as diverse as the colors of a farmer's market. Some folks battle diabetes, others have unique dietary needs—the list goes on. That's why having a plethora of grocery stores scattered across every city to choose from is a blessing. I mix and match my shopping destinations. A little from here, a little from there—it's like creating a culinary symphony of savings!

In this land of opportunity, stores determine what price they'll slap on their products, sometimes a price variation that could rival a roller coaster ride. Your mission? Seek out the best bang for your buck. Be a savvy shopper, a price detective on a mission to conquer the grocery aisles.

USDA Organic vs. Non-GMO

Let's decipher the code, shall we? USDA stands for the "United States Department of Agriculture" and they are responsible for the "USDA Organic" label that is found on some foods (though these foods may still contain organic sugar). On the other hand, non-GMO signifies that the food is free from genetically modified organisms, but not necessarily organic. Still with me, here?

The USDA Organic certification ensures that the product has been produced using approved methods that promote ecological balance, conserve biodiversity, avoiding synthetic fertilizers, pesticides, genetically modified organisms (GMOs), and certain other substances. It also involves practices that promote the well-being of livestock, such as access to the outdoors and organic feed.

It's important to note that the USDA Organic certification specifically pertains to agricultural products and does not cover non-food items or aspects such as packaging, processing methods, or fair-trade practices. Different countries may have their own organic certification programs, but the USDA Organic seal is specific to the United States.

Keep an eye out for those mysterious fruit and vegetable stickers. If the five-digit number starts with a 9, it's organic. If it starts with a 4, well, it's not. Now it's up to you to decide if the organic route is worth the extra green in your wallet.

Even when it comes to organics, I urge you to remain vigilant. Yes, even with those seemingly pure and pristine packaged goodies, labels remain your ally. Read, read, and read some more, for within those lines lie the secrets of what truly goes into your favorite dishes and your body…

So, my fellow gastronomes, heed my warnings of quality, price fluctuations, and the sugar and sodium-filled surprises that await you. Armed with knowledge and a discerning eye, embark on.

And remember, healthy eating is all about balance and moderation. Don't be too hard on yourself if you occasionally indulge in a treat or eat something that's not 100% healthy. The key is to make healthy choices most of the time, and to enjoy your food!

Quick Tips

- **Check out local farmers' markets:** If you're looking for fresh, local produce, check out farmers' markets in your area. These markets often have a variety of fruits and vegetables that are in season, and you can talk to the local farmers about their growing practices. You can also find artisanal cheeses, breads, and other locally made products at these markets. Not only can you find fresh and often locally grown produce at farmers' markets, but you can also support local farmers and businesses.

- **Use online grocery delivery services:** Many grocery stores now offer online ordering and delivery, which can save you time and money if you want to avoid impulse purchases.

- **Use price comparison websites/apps:** Websites like flip.com and apps like Basket allow you to compare prices across multiple grocery stores so you can find the best deal.

- **Consider joining a co-op or buying club:** Co-ops and buying clubs are membership-based organizations that allow members to buy food in bulk at discounted prices.
- **Use coupons and loyalty programs:** Many grocery stores have loyalty programs and coupons that can help you save money.
- **Be aware of food waste:** The US has a significant problem with food waste, so consider buying only what you need and using up leftovers to reduce waste.
- **Consider food safety:** The US has strict food safety regulations, but it's still important to handle and store food properly to avoid foodborne illnesses.
- **Finding the products you want:** If you're looking for a specific brand or product, you can search for it online before going to the store. Many grocery stores have their inventory available online or in an app, so you can see if they carry the products you're looking for. You can also use apps like Instacart or Amazon Fresh to have groceries delivered to you from various stores.
- **Organic vs. non-GMO:** While organic and non-GMO are not the same thing, they often overlap. Organic foods are grown without the use of synthetic pesticides or fertilizers, and they are not genetically modified. Non-GMO foods, on the other hand, are not genetically modified, but they may not be organic. If you're concerned about both pesticides and GMOs, look for products that are labeled both USDA organic and non-GMO.

- **Added sugar:** Sugar can be found in many unexpected products, including condiments, dressings, and sauces. When reading labels, look for ingredients like high fructose corn syrup, cane sugar, and molasses. If you're trying to limit your sugar intake, aim for products with less than 5 grams of added sugar per serving.

- **Added sodium:** Sodium is a common ingredient found in various food products, often added for flavor enhancement and preservation. It can be present in surprising sources such as soups, snacks, and processed meats. When examining food labels, be on the lookout for terms like sodium chloride, monosodium glutamate (MSG), and sodium bicarbonate. To manage your sodium intake, it is recommended to choose products with less than 140 milligrams of added sodium per serving, especially if you are monitoring your salt consumption for dietary reasons.

- **Discount stores:** If you're on a budget, consider shopping at discount stores. They may have a more limited selection, however, you can still find healthy options like fresh produce, lean proteins, and whole grains at these stores.

Helpful Websites

Remember to check if these platforms are available in your specific location, as availability may vary. Additionally, consider using grocery store loyalty cards and apps provided by individual stores, as they often have exclusive discounts and offers.

- https://flipp.com
- https://basket.app
- https://www.instacart.com
- https://www.amazon.com/fresh
- https://thrivemarket.com

CONCLUSION

Congratulations on embarking on this exciting new chapter of your life! In this guide, we've covered everything you need to know to start right, save time, and avoid costly mistakes.

By following these steps, you'll be well on your way to building a solid foundation for your new life in the land of plenty. And remember, the journey doesn't end here; it's just the beginning of an incredible adventure filled with endless possibilities.

As you immerse yourself in the American experience and forge new connections, keep a positive mindset and approach every challenge with enthusiasm. Everyone can find their place in the United States, and that's what makes this country so great.

Remember, you have the power to shape your destiny and create the life you've always dreamed of.

Now go forth and conquer! May your journey be filled with joy, success, and unforgettable moments as you settle in and make America your new home.

Happy settling!

Your friend,

Susie Lavender

Printed in Great Britain
by Amazon